I0481125

JSGN-OSHN

The Ultimate Guide For Career
Enhancement

How to GET PROMOTED At Work

**Master The Art Of Living A Corporate
Life, Achieve Your Goals, Get
Recognized, And Accelerate Your
Corporate Career.**

Author
Mr. Swapnil P. Modi
**LL.M. (Business Laws - Gold Medalist),
LL.B. (General - Gold Medalist)
and M.B.A. (HR)**

Warning

The content contained within this book may not be reproduced, duplicated or copied by whatever means, modes or manner, or storing, printing or transmitting in any form, any part of this book without the prior written consent of the author will entail both the civil and criminal action without any further notice. This book is copyright protected and it is for personal use only.

Under no circumstances will any blame or legal responsibility be held against the author or publisher (if any) for any damages, reparation or monetary loss due to the information contained within this book either directly or indirectly.

Table of Contents

Acknowledgements

This book is my sincere endeavor to put in one place all the hacks of scaling up one's professional career, though compiling vast information on these topics is an impossible task but I have put in my reasonable best efforts to incorporate essential elements that are required to climb up your career ladder.

I am sincerely thankful to the following people who played an important role by taking me ahead in the journey of writing this book:

First and foremost, my countless thanks to the ALMIGHTY GOD, for always backing me up and making things possible with your intangible unconditional support.

I am deeply thankful of the blessings that my father late Shri. Prafulkumar Natawarlal Modi has bestowed upon me and I am acutely thankful to my loving mother Kashmira Chotubhai

Rakhashia for her constant love & support and my younger brother Vicky Prafulkumar Modi.

I shall always be grateful to Advocate Krishna S., the one who again inspired me to write this book, and for being my first reader and giving me continuous constructive feedback in completing this book.

Thank you, thank you, thank you to my designer, Marmie S., for your creative vision in designing the beautiful covers for all my books.

My thanks also go out to my mentors and my management team for their unmatched support, without your support I would have not reached to this level.

Also, my friends without you, my life is incomplete.

Thank you everyone for always believing in me and giving me your blessings and enormous love. I am blessed to have you all in my life.

Suggestions are most welcome from my readers and nothing in this book is meant in any way to offend anyone either expressly or impliedly.

I again take this opportunity to communicate with all working professionals and give them a simple message:

****

"Bring passion in your work that you love your work and can"t resist it."

***

"Time and again, give yourself a goal of getting promoted to a next level and make your corporate journey more exciting."

***

"Prepare the plan of action to meet your goals and stay focused until you accomplish it."

****

Prologue

Admit it, you must have thought of this (at least once): why the same individual is being promoted every year or alternate year or as and when the promotion occurs as per your company policy? Whereas, I am sure that you have also noticed some working professionals are stuck at the same level (I mean at the job title) for years (in some cases this may extend up to 4-5 years) and they aren't being promoted to the next level. If yes, then have you thought of the different possibilities to increase your performance to scale up the career ladder at work? And if you have mentally accepted your existing job title and its associated responsibilities, then that's all you'd get and you won't get any additional responsibilities as you aren't prepared for it. Some people are perfectly happy staying in the same role/job title for their entire career, and they don't want to advance up their career ladder. Everybody wants to move up but only a few are able to step-up, do you know **why?** It's a matter of personal preference and the choices you make, and if you are happy with current scenario even if your paycheck is low but if you have mentally accepted it then you won't put any extra efforts to change it. It is completely your choice; if you think about it for once then you'd be bombarded with lots of interconnected questions and thoughts related to that one point which you had consciously thought of. *What if I say:* **YES! You can -GET PROMOTED at your work**." In other words, I'd rather say: ***Yes! You can scale up your career ladder & get promoted at your work***. *How does that sound?*

I have encountered many professionals in my 15+ years of corporate experience and one thing I can say, that every individual is not a born entrepreneur, off-course with no offence to those who are. However, I had noticed that there are huge numbers of professionals who either love their work or they have developed their comfort zone and don't wish to break their own created limitations and they pretend to love their work even if they don't. Their corporate life revolves around that tiny circle so called as their comfort zone and they are happy with it. They have   lost the desire to step out of their comfort zone and take new challenges.

There could be many reasons, and few of those are:

- ✓ They don't like their job.
- ✓ They don't wish to any take risk. (Often people are afraid of taking new challenges.)
- ✓ They like to continue the way they are operating and remain in their comfort zone unless a new task is assigned to them out of their will.
- ✓ They have built a rapport in their organization over a period of time which they don't want to lose. After all it takes a decent time to build trust and they don't wish to take a risk of losing it should they fail in the newly assigned task.
- ✓ They don't wish to Ancash their goodwill and join new employer and start building a new rapport from scratch.
- ✓ They have a family commitment that carries more priorities than taking risk of learning and mastering new skills and undertake addition responsibilities.

✓ They have financial commitments and don't wish to put all of those at a *STAKE* by entering into managerial mindset.

Ask yourself, are you connected with your work? Do you love your work? Or task(s) that you are performing at your work? Or are you living your corporate life or just going through it?

If you don't love your work or don't feel like going to the work then you aren't connected with your work and if you aren't connected, then you are only working for the sake of working in the incorrect environment and spoiling the important years of your life. This might sound harsh but if that's the case, then I urge you to find a job that interest you the most so you can excel in your work and scale up your career ladder in the near future otherwise you are only wasting your time.

As you read through this book, you may feel there is too much information on what to do and how to proceed further. I request that you pick what you like in this book first, and then complete that task to move to another task and keep moving forward.

This book consists of ideas and suggestions to help improve your understanding of the corporate culture and grow in your career.

#The Goal of this book

Thanks for taking up this book. Glad to see you here! The goal of this book is to teach you some of the highly effective principles and methods used by corporate professionals and they got promoted to the next rank or next job title at their work in the corporate world. The book provides solutions to augment your current role; build your confidence and imbibe happiness in your work. My hope is that my book will inspire you to set another goal or dream a new dream or create a life you love and rise in your professional career.

#Who is this book for?

This book is a manifestation of years' long observation of corporate environment and its culture. Therefore, this book shall be helpful to all the aspiring managers & leaders who have ever wished to get promoted at their work. Remember, perseverance and consistencies are the keys to success. On regular workdays, most of our time (*of-course after deducting the sleeping hours*) is spent at our work. I have personally observed many professionals living their life under an unfitted work environment. Either they don't like their work or they not completely satisfied with their work. Despite this, they spend their life's important years doing ill-suited jobs without realizing the need of the scaling up their role to bring back the excitement at work. The reason could be: either they have not succeeded in their goal in past so they dropped it, or they haven't thought of it ever or they've thought of it however, they would have lost the interest and got distracted or they couldn't prepare the correct plan of action to meet their goals which lead to the failure or distractions and ultimately they've lost their hopes of getting promoted to the next rank at their work.

In other words, right where you are, you can take on development and leadership positions and obtain the expertise you need to prepare for the senior level job for which you are dreaming of. Hence, before actually undertaking the responsibility to run an entire division, you can take a mentoring position or a team lead position or head up a small project, or even do some volunteering to get management experience. So when you're part of the group and not the current leader, this will give you the time to develop your skills and evolve. Do the extra work now and your consistent efforts will make you the better winner as opportunities arises in the near future, and the best part is, by then you're prepared for it.

Remember, there is a purpose behind our every act and omission. Take action to scale up your potential and enhance your career. How your day flows will determine how your work flows and ultimately it determines how you climb-up your career ladder.

Let's look at some of the strategies in detail that need to be followed to fulfill your dream of climbing the corporate ladder and getting promoted at work. This will not only allow you to stay more focused and motivated but will create a spark within you that encourages you to achieve your career goals.

Ch:1 The Beginning

1.1 <u>Knowing Yourself</u>

—Observing yourself is the necessary starting point for any real change.
—Chalmers Brothers

One of the fundamentals of self-confidence is to understand your "strengths;" not being able to consider your own myths could put you on the path to low self-esteem. Become a person that "takes in the positive," listens to praise and find skills that could be clues to your talents. Here's an example: your colleague tells you that she likes your dressing sense and is impressed with your business attire. What the hell are you going to do with that understanding? Similarly, knowing your weaknesses will make it possible for you to be true to yourself and others on what you're not good at. You may intend to either concentrate on these flaws to improve it or try to make them a minor part of your job or your personal life.

The first and foremost step to bring in some real transformation is to observe yourself. Let's do a little routine to do just that. Keep your pen and paper handy, please. Believe me, the words written with a pen on every sheet of paper make your mind vibrate, and you seem to remember better than any other format. Back to our point, what I meant was to recognize and list your personality, your ability, and your main strengths. Only think about all the things you've learned in the past year. Then I also would like you to list the other skills/areas that you think improvement is needed, and last but not least, I want you to also understand the importance of those skills that you do not possess, but you are keen to learn and master. In the same way, draw on the current abilities that you learn and the new skills that your future role in your organization needs. Identify your competence scorecard and be willing to take a step towards mastering the new skill to compete for the new task. Once you've written all of this, take a close look at your responses, you'll see the skills that demand your commitment to improve and learn it. These are all the skills that will help you succeed throughout your career.

As a result, you'll have a good understanding of your established skills and the things you're doing in your current job.

However, the crucial question remains: why do we want to understand ourselves in the first place? There are a few leading theories for this:

1. **Mindfulness**

   Humans are a varied and complex species. We must become more self-aware in a variety of ways in order to become more self-aware. Our personality traits, personal values, behaviors, desires, and the social factors that affect our behavior are all important aspects of self-awareness.

2. **Character**

   Usually, we don't change the way we hear about ourselves, based on what we believe and really need. Knowing our personalities will nevertheless help us recognize scenarios in which we are successful and help us avoid situations with too much conflict. For example, if you are a highly reserved person, you are likely to feel more stress in your sales job than a highly extroverted person might have experienced. And I'm sure you've observed most of the sales people who aren't really going to give up when it comes to concluding a deal. At times, their consistent follow-ups help them sell their services and products. On the other hand, an introvert can quickly give up and not chase the way an extrovert does with his customers. So, if you are highly introverted, you should either learn skills to cope with the demands of an extrovert interpersonal position, or you should find a role that is more compatible with your personal viewpoint.

3. Principles

It is important for each and every one of us to consider and rely on our personal values. For example, if your first focus is "being there for your children" or "your relationship with the love of your life" or "expanding your company," it is very possible to lose sight of those priorities on a day-to-day, moment-by-moment basis. Too many problems and opportunities arise during the working day that our "things to do" lists will soon overwhelm the time we have to do them. Since little (if any) of these things pertain to what we love the most, it's possible to spend a lot of time on lower priority projects. When we focus on our values, we are more inclined to accomplish what we believe to be the most important.

4. Practices

Our behaviors are routines that are repeated constantly and often unintentionally. Although we would like to have habits that help us work effectively with and influence others, we should still consider at least one of our habits that hinder our effectiveness. For example, if you are a boss who never consults with your team before making decisions, the approach could be at conflicts with your desire to build up your staff's commitment to judgments and decision-making skills.

5. Desires

Well-known experts including Maslow and others have identified a variety of psychological needs that inspire our behavior, such as the need for recognition, affection, belonging, achievement, self-realization, power and control. One of the advantages of knowing who has the most impact on our own decisions is the opportunity to realize how it influences our interpersonal relationships. For example, most of us have certainly met people who are in high need of status. They are attracted to high-level careers and perform high-level positions within their organizations. They also like to get things that symbolize their status. They focus on showing loyalty, and they want benefits and privileges that those of lower status can't afford. Some people, too, are fighting for something that some see as inconsequential — like a greater workplace. Needs cause motivation; and when needs are not fulfilled, they may cause frustration, conflict, and stress.

6. Philosophical self-awareness

It has recently been a hot topic of discussion because it is one of the five facets of emotional intelligence. Understanding your own feelings, what causes them, and how they affect your thoughts and behavior is emotional self-awareness. If you've always been excited about your career, but not excited right now, are you going to get excited again? In order to address the challenge, it helps to understand the internal processes associated with excitement. That sounds clearer than that. Here's an analogy: I guess I know how to start my car—-I put the gas in the tank, put the key in the ignition, and turn the key. But, my mechanic knows a lot more about what's going on in order to get my car started than I do—he knows what's going on under the hood. My mechanic has the ability to start my car at times when   I'm not because he knows the internal processes. Similarly, a person with a high degree of emotional self-awareness understands the internal structure of emotional perception and, thus, the process of self-awareness.

7. Self-knowledge

It is closely related to one of our basic needs, our need to perceive and make sense of our experience. This means learning as many of our own patterns, desires, and mechanisms as possible. As in other disciplines, the more we understand, the more we will discover. And who doesn't want to be the master of his own house.

8. Confusion is the reverse of self-knowledge

How we really are, our true intentions, our deeper patterns, and how we see ourselves. Self-knowledge eliminates a gap between our self-perception and how others see us. Delusive assessment of our abilities and qualities, in the sense of "unrecognized arrogance," can be a source of great embarrassment when unmasked. If our understanding of ourselves is founded on strong ground, we will expend a great deal of our energy defending our self-image against the threat of cognitive dissonance. Because we have a wide-ranging things to cover and a lot to lose, we're going to find it hard to communicate with anyone authentically and honestly.

9. Freud would say that self-knowledge liberates us from being a slave to our unconscious and its many almost irrational urges. And if we know our patterns and where they come from, we'd be able to tackle them efficiently. Understanding our history stops us from blindly repeating unproductive habits of the past. It may also lead to a kinder, more compassionate view of what we can see as our failures.

10. Essentially, self-knowledge enables one to be more diligent in response to

potential events. If we truly know our behaviors, our causes, and our desires, and if we have the emotional maturity to consider our feelings because they are, we are much less likely to be controlled by them.

11. In the end, self-knowledge is always the first step needed to facilitate positive change. And by taking stock of what is – as objective as possible – we prepare ourselves for the tomorrow's challenges and work on what we want to change and make strides against it.

1.2 How Self-Awareness Makes You More Effective

> — Maybe other people will try to limit me, but I don't limit myself.
>
> — Jim Carrey

Self-awareness enables managers to recognize gaps in their operational expertise that promote the development of skills. But self-awareness also allows managers to recognize environments in which they are most competitive, to aid intuitive decision-making, and to help maintain tension, and to empower themselves and others.

1. **Knowledge expansion**. In certain cases, improvement programs should begin with a comparison of the current condition to the desired future state. When you have a clear picture of who you are, you will figure out what you need to do to make your life simpler. Self-awareness will also reveal a flaw in the skills you want to improve.

2. **Identifying your strengths and weaknesses**. Self-awareness enables you to capitalize on your strengths while also addressing your weaknesses. When making significant decisions, for example, if you are good at "seeing the big picture" that surrounds decisions but not so good at focusing on details, you might want to consult with colleagues and subordinates who are more detail-oriented. Collaboration between big-picture thinkers and detail-oriented thinkers will result in high-quality decisions.

3. **Increasing instinctive decision making skills**. Members with a high level of relational self-awareness make more intuitive decisions. In complex situations, subjective decision-makers examine large amounts of unstructured and ambiguous facts and choose a course of action based on a "gut instinct" or "sense" of what is right. If the rate of transition, the degree of uncertainty, and

the complexity of their market environment increase, this type of decision-making becomes more critical for managers. Managers who are highly aware of their emotions are more able to read their "gut feelings" and use them to guide decisions.

4. **Tension.** Job that doesn't suit your personality seems to give you more stress than work that does.

5. **Inspiration**. It's very hard to live with bad results, when you don't understand what affects them. You'll feel powerless if you don't know what behaviors you need to change to improve your performance. Self-awareness is motivating when it reveals that performance issues exist and what can be done to improve performance.   Furthermore, understanding your psychological needs will boost your motivation by encouraging you to value and seek opportunities that you genuinely want, such as a sense of accomplishment,

greater responsibility, the opportunity to help others, or a flexible work schedule.

6. **Leadership.** When we consider "what makes us tick" what makes us excited, why we behave as we do, and so on, we even gain insight into what makes others tick. To the point that other people are like you (and, of course, there are exceptions to similarity), learning how to encourage you is equal to understanding how to inspire others.

1.3 **Prepare Your Personal/Individual Development Plan First**

Self-knowledge simply increases our chances of making smarter choices. It turns us into better pilots in our lives, granting us mastery and realism as well as congruence and alignment. It's going to make us more humble, too. In reality, as Socrates well understood, a vital part of self-knowledge is to know what we do not know, and to readily admit our ignorance. Self-knowledge, is not about coming face to face with what's off with us and being stuck with it. It's about having to wake up to what's right and right about us right down to the core, giving it our full attention, trying to grasp the full dimension of this point of view, and allowing it to transform us.

Now is the time to draft an IDP (Individual Development Plan) for yourself, when you have identified yourself, your abilities and your strengths. Please remember, the incentives are the exact proportion of the value you bring to the manager on the table (you may deem this as your compensation). Therefore, reflecting your real status is how your current earnings are, and if you wish to increase your earnings and climb up your career ladder, you need to include additional values to optimize rewards.

Summary:

If things are coming easy and you are getting comfortable, you are getting trapped into survival mode because the short term pleasures can lead to long term traps of getting stuck at same level with same role or job title. This is not to suggest that you can never take a position that is in contrast with your personality. However, be mindful that you're going to have to work extra hard to build skills for that job, because there are jobs that will become less stressful for you. Identify your strengths and your needs as desires sometimes acts as a motivating factor to take action.

Ch:2 The Empowerment

—You get what you settle for.

– Thelma and Louise

Your mind is an incredible thing or rather I'd say it's an incredible gift given by almighty GOD, built to learn and feel everything present in this so called universe. You have what is called neuroplasticity, the brain's ability to change and react according to its environment and chromosomes. Depending on your experiences, your brain is going to create new neural relations, and it can be very easy. That's how phobias happen, if you've burnt your tongue with an extremely hot coffee in past, then you are most likely to let your coffee cool down before you drink it. That's how our brain identified stuffs from prior experiences and sends a signal so we can act accordingly.

In reality, according to others, it takes about twenty-one days for a person to break or develop a new habit that would feel comfortable doing something different after a certain amount of time. To some point, I agree with this, since some problems can be very easy to modify in my experience, while others take a little more repetition; which could take more than 21 days too. You can see how resilient the brain can be if you can grow a phobia from just one bad experience. It can take three weeks to degrade a strong neuronal kit in the brain and replace it with the kind of habit that you really need, but with the proper urge, change can be random.

This quotation is from Janis Joplin, who argued that you cannot settle for anything other than what makes you happy. If you do, that's exactly what you become. At some stage, everybody has to compromise for something. You can't get it all, and you can't carry on without compromising your whole life. However, you're not just supposed to settle for less than what makes you happy. Instead of doing what you think is the right thing to do, you know you have what you need as happiness follows.

It's a funny term when you think about it. Settle is defined as stopping and staying in one place and putting it in order, arranging or fixing it   as necessary. To me, the word suggests that you no longer want to make new discoveries, that you sit in the same position, maybe with the same person or individual, and that you refrain from doing new things or seeking out different things. Same theory applies at your work environment, if you continue to sit in the same position and carry same job duties then you are likely to miss the opportunities of growth in your career. Likewise, you will miss all the excitement of work and slowly you are likely to lose your interest towards your work and you start developing a feeling of dissatisfaction. It's mainly because repetition and lack of variation makes us feel low at times. As said by the experts, only change is constant. So take charge of your life, personal and professional to make the quality of your life improved from what it is at present.

2.1 <u>Excel in your existing role and get noticed by finding a mentor for yourself and becoming one for someone</u>.

> **—Pearls don't lie on the seashore. If you want one, you must dive for it.**
> **— Chinese proverb**

Mentors are considered as vital elements to the advancement of the career. They will expose you to new viewpoints and perspectives. It is necessary to have a coach at work to achieve new skills and knowledge. A good mentor will help you navigate some of the challenges and roadblocks that you face. Right trainers will help you figure out the next steps that align with you and help you navigate challenges that fall right in your blind spot. They guide you based upon their knowledge and experience of their forte and you don't have to spent that many years to go through all of those failures if you have a chosen a right mentor.

Those people who tell you what you need to know, not what you want to learn, will be wonderful teachers. They're going to give you the real advice you need to fill in the blind holes that will put you in a position to move ahead.

Similarly, looking for a suitable mentor or dream about getting a good mentor should be your primary goal if you wish to accomplish your goals in the right time. In certain ways, taking the next step in your career means that you're going to have to deal with people. It's the best way to train someone and to be a mentor to someone. You should act as a mentor at work, you should think a lot about inspiring people and ask them to be optimistic.

When it comes to practicing and learning a new skill, I've experimented with hundreds of different tips, tricks and tips. There is a theme that stands out. When it comes to mastering a new skill, the most important advice is to find a coach or a trainer.

But don't just take someone. Get anyone, the best you can afford, who's very good at coaching. Ensure that the person you chose for coaching has mastered their skills in the hard way. More importantly, assess their track record, ensuring that the coach has successfully taught people in the past, the same thing you're trying to do.

Once you have identified & elected the correct mentor and you are firm on your decision of getting trained under his mentorship, talk to that person. Express your interest and your goals and be absolute transparent with all the facts. Remember, if you hide your weaknesses then it becomes difficult for you to overcome it even with the help of the right mentor. Instead, share your strengths and weaknesses with your mentor and seek advice on overcoming your flaws so you can accomplish your goal and attain success.

2.2   <u>Increase your credibility</u>

—The question isn't who is going to let me; it's who is going to stop me.

– Ayn Rand

Meet representatives of other departments, other organizations, and other teams. Be inquisitive about your department. Know what you can about their work and their skills. Check out if they have the ability to see if, in your free time, you'd be able to step in to develop the skills you'd like to use to enhance your career.

There are also benefits when it comes to teaching. In general, you are making strides on the basis of an explicitly prepared plan that has already been effective for others. They see the weakest thing you can do is educate the incorrectly. A good coach means you're really at the forefront of your skills. They know how to properly interact with the practice. You'll get quick feedback on the progress and outcomes. You're already being pushed in the right direction by them. They will make you their dream mentor.

2.3   Build trust & confidence

"If you think you can do a thing or think you can't do a thing, you're right.

– Henry Ford

Control freaks, you need to pay special attention to this one. You are tasked not only with your own duties as a supervisor, but also with the supervision of others. With the extra level of responsibility, you just don't have the time to work on something that needs to be done independently. And you're going to have to remember how to move that when the time comes.

Career coach Angela Copeland says, "It's important to get things done as a boss through the delegation." You need to learn how to let things go and support your team. And, you have to believe, encourage, and trust them more than anything else. Those who claim that they have a supportive supervisor who expects them to get the job done are the happiest employees.

2.4 <u>Train your jr and show your appreciation to encourage him to do more.</u>

—If you do what you've always done, you'll get what you've always gotten.

— Tony Robbins

All of us have standard 24 hours in a day, and regardless of our efficiency, our performance is reduced if we do it all on our own. Learn to take up additional duties from your seniors and equally discharge any of your responsibilities to your juniors. Teach them the skills they need to complete this challenge and scale up their ability. Thus, by learning how to maximize, you will still profit from a proportion of other people's contributions, and hopefully the management will notice it.

Prepare and share the IDP (Individual Development Plan) with the team or junior members. Discuss the action plan and let him or her know that you're there to help him or her in his or her development. Remember, the benefits (you can deem your compensation) are in the exact proportion of the benefit you contribute to your employer's table. Therefore, whatever your present earnings are, is the reflective of your actual jobs, and if you want to ramp up your earnings and step-up your career ladder, you need to offer additional values to maximize your earnings.

2.5   Become confident and kill your hesitation because:

—It's hard to beat a person who never gives up.

— Babe Ruth

The brightest of us are saying that success is only beyond our comfort zone. It goes without saying, however, that you must extend into your sphere of competence. Believe me, once you're optimistic, you've already completed your 50 percent of the ride, and you're emotionally trained to complete the rest. It's all about our thinking.

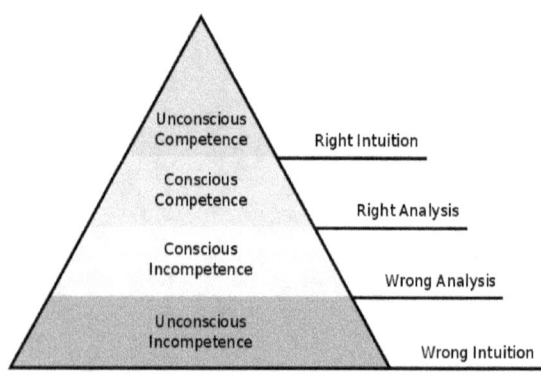

Hierarchy of Competence

Management trainer **Martin M. Broadwell** described the model as "the four levels of teaching" in February 1969. **Paul R. Curtiss and Phillip W. Warren** mentioned the model in their 1973 book: -*The Dynamics of Life Skills Coaching.* The model was used at Gordon Training International by its employee Noel Burch in the 1970s; there it was called the "*four stages for learning any new skill.*"

When you enter the conscious incompetence you have to face the dip.

There are five main reasons why you might quit when you find yourself deep in the dip:

1. *You run out of time*
2. *You run out of money*
3. *You get scared*
4. *You"re not serious about it*
5. *You lose interest*

Make sure that doesn't happen to you.

The four stages mean that people are originally oblivious of how little or unconscious they feel of their incompetence. Recognizing their ignorance, they deliberately learn a talent, and then consciously use it. Eventually, abilities can be used without being deliberately thought through: the person is said to have gained implicit competence after that.

The four stages are:

1. **Unconscious incompetence**

   The client does not understand or know how to do it and does not necessarily accept the shortfall. They could dispute the utility of the ability. The participant must understand his or her own incompetence and the worth of the new talent before going on to the next level. The amount of time a person spends at this point depends on the extent of his desire to learn.

2. **Conscious incompetence**

   While individuals do not understand or know how to do anything, they consider the deficit as well as the importance of a new ability to solve the deficit. Having errors may be an important part of the learning experience at this point.

3. **Conscious competence**

   The person understands or knows how to do something about it. However, the demonstration of talent or experience involves attention. It can be broken down into stages, and there is a strong conscious participation in the execution of the new abilities.

4. **Unconscious competence**

The leaned expert has had so much experience in the ability that it has become his "second nature" and the task assigned to him can be done effortlessly. As a consequence, the skill may be performed while doing another mission. The expert will be able to teach it to others, based on how and when it has been taught.

Keep the excitement on in your personal as well as in your professional life. Believe me, corporate life is really an enjoyable ride of professional life, if you slightly adjust the way you look at the things.

Summary

It's time to bring the revised edition to the forefront. Make the best of your potential and start taking initiative. If you don't use your potential, you lose it. If you don't take initiative at the right moment, you'll soon end up with what you have, because you won't be able to get out of your comfort zone that easily in future too if you can't step out of your comfort zone right now. Eventually, you will be putting the same efforts either it's today or its tomorrow, the decision is absolutely yours. Don't get stuck in a position that you're not faced with options, because if you've had to thrive in that world, you've had to exist on whoever you've been allocated to. Take care of your life, your status, your job description before someone else takes it.

Ch:3 The Goal Setting

—If you don't build your dream, someone else will hire you to help them build theirs.

— Dhirubhai Ambani

It's time for you to get selfish and figure out exactly what you want. Try setting goals for yourself. Master a few skills before you get there, if you intend to do some work. And just dreaming about your assignments will not make it easier for you to complete them unless you act on it. Mind habits will get you closer to where you want your life to be, according to Psychology Today. Apparently, many athletes have been using this technique for years to boost their performance. To get started, set your goals and presume that you have already achieved that objective in the future. Try to immerse yourself fully in this situation as you imagine it. This pattern of thinking may be coupled with consultation or positive assertions. In your new lifestyle, this is a step that lets you envision yourself and it will be easier for you to accept it as it finally happens.

3.1 <u>Define your goals</u>

—Success is most often achieved by those who don't know that failure is inevitable.

– Coco Chanel

Goal visualization is the first step towards progress. However, your action plays an important part in meeting your targets. If you have agreed to be elevated, you must be mindful that your next position/title needs you to support and assist your team mates to accomplish their goals.

Find more among the team-mates who are unable to keep up with their workload. Donate your time and suggestions to help them out. Don't take credit here, or lose the confidence of your colleagues. Know that your contribution and mood will be noticed. It will be better for them to consider your leadership before your team recognizes you, or until you are out-of-turned.

Tell your loved ones about the changes you're making to keep your life on track. When you start getting the positive vibes out, it's going to come back to you at full force. Let both of you do the exactly what you're going to do. If they know why and how you're going to change your life for the better, your peers are going to influence and help you.

Deepak Chopra said, according to The Huffington Post, "*Anything worth having only increases when it is given.*" You are unsure about sharing your thoughts and passions, but it will make you stronger and help you stay inspired and focused on your journey.

Recognizing the expectations that have been posed will increase your progress early in your career and accelerate the achievement of goals. Then, if you can get tasks ahead of your current position and pay grade, you set yourself up for early promotions, higher promotions and more bonuses (in other words you can say: incentives or commissions).

3.2 <u>Divide your goals</u>

—Don't judge each day by the harvest you reap but by the seeds that you plant.

– Robert Louis Stevenson

Write your yearly goals, half-yearly goals, quarterly goals, and monthly goals. Divide your goals into 4 categories and write it down on a sheet of paper/on your diary:

Timeline v/s Goals
Annually ➔
Half-yearly ➔
Quarterly ➔
Monthly ➔

This will help you keep yourself motivated as now you can see that all your goals are categorized properly and slowly and gradually you are working towards the fulfillment of your goals.

There is a psychological justification to divide the priorities into frequent timelines, such as short-term goals and long-term goals. For example, if you just write down your long-term objectives, it might take a little longer to achieve your target, because there are improvements that you might get diverted from and losing confidence in meeting your long-term goals. In the other hand, if you write short-term targets that can be reached over a shorter period of time than your short-term goals, your morale can be lifted to the next level. Again, you're working on another short-term target, and that's how you're starting to reach the intermediate objectives that are needed to achieve your long-term goal. This will help you commit to your occasional long-term target and, in exchange, you will not lose your concentration on reaching your objectives.

Hold on a second and pause for a little while and, we've been applying the same technique since childhood in our studies, playing cricket, and even in our high school and college days.

Initially, we'll give ourselves a shorter target, once we achieve it, we'll take another one and finally hit the final goal. The same approach is applied to our educational institutions.

However, their main objective is to train you for handle the situation that occurs in the real life by preparing you for the final test; to gain morale and keep you in control, they will prepare you for the unit test, internal term tests, and occasional tests, including a surprise test too. It's all to make sure you don't lose track, because the faster you start getting positive grades in these initial tests, your trust level has increased, and you're all set to appear and take part in the annual & final exam.

Same principle is applied by the gym trainer or any fitness trainer. Initially he'll ask you to do warm-up your body for 10-15 minutes and then will allow you to do the workout for 30 minutes. That's it for that day! Now, once your body has adapted the workout schedule then you will be allowed to increase your workout timings and permitted to perform other workout exercises in the gym.

As a result, a proper division of your priorities through a proper quarterly timetable is incredibly necessary to meet your ideal long-term goals.

3.3 <u>Guarantee a Better Picture</u>

−<u>**Repeatedly accomplish major achievements**</u>.

A single success can be considered as your fortune, but sustained success can only be attained by mastering the challenge and achieving success repeatedly time and again. Make sure the team and executives are aware that you are working on a larger project. Increase your credibility in your new role. In order to meet standards, act according to a timetable. Let your boss know that you're ready for more once you've won his confidence. It may sound selfish, but all you have to do is try to focus on yourself when you turn around and not worry about what other people will think. Whatever you do, it's easier said than done. Just because someone else's journey is effective doesn't mean you have to follow in their footsteps. According to Elite Daily, people will continue to have their thoughts, but if you continue to make choices based on what others say, you will become stuck. Break your thought pattern and do what you feel is best for you.

3.4 <u>Create a list of your top priorities.</u>

—Start Earlier and Work Harder

In such a similar note, the minimal bandwidth and manpower you would have as a boss will find it crucial to consider the most critical activities that must be attended to first.

You will be asked to take on more responsibility than you actually do, and your team has the time to do so. -The ability to delegate projects will help you succeed in your management career. This will empower you to set realistic goals for your boss, shielding your workers from exhaustion.

You can start your shift a little earlier if possible, or you can stretch your shift a little longer if the situation calls for it. This will assist you in completing your assignments within the allotted time and without a terrible backlog.

As I have explained in my previous book, -Time Management acts as an important factor especially in managerial roles.

3.5 <u>Track your work</u>.

Could you track all the additional activities you've perform in previous year? Don't worry, from now, yes you can! Use this tracker cum checklist prepared for tracking additional activities annually. Capture a screenshot of the below *ADDITIONAL* **activities checklist (annual)** and take a print out and check each of these options upon completing that task and repeat this process for 12 months and you'd see the results.

Checklist for tracking *Additional* activities performed in a year

Annual Activity Tracker For Year 20____

Sr.	Total task /timeline	Monthly			Quarterly		Half-yearly		Annually
1.	Provided new suggestion for process improvement	Jan □ Apr □ Jul □ Oct □	Feb □ May □ Aug □ Nov □	Mar □ Jun □ Sep □ Dec □	Q1 (jfm) □ Q2 (amj) □ Q3 (jas) □ Q4 (ond) □		Jan-jun □ Jul-dec □		Jan – dec □
2.	Interacted with other team members, built a rapport with them and/or offered help & assistance when required.	Jan □ Apr □ Jul □ Oct □	Feb □ May □ Aug □ Nov □	Mar □ Jun □ Sep □ Dec □	Q1 (jfm) □ Q2 (amj) □ Q3 (jas) □ Q4 (ond) □		Jan-jun □ Jul-dec □		Jan – dec □
3.	Conducted training (if permitted) or requested to conduct training for juniors or new joinies or a refresher training for existing team member.	Jan □ Apr □ Jul □ Oct □	Feb □ May □ Aug □ Nov □	Mar □ Jun □ Sep □ Dec □	Q1 (jfm) □ Q2 (amj) □ Q3 (jas) □ Q4 (ond) □		Jan-jun □ Jul-dec □		Jan – dec □
4.	Offered help to the existing team members in achieving their targets	Jan □ Apr □ Jul □ Oct □	Feb □ May □ Aug □ Nov □	Mar □ Jun □ Sep □ Dec □	Q1 (jfm) □ Q2 (amj) □ Q3 (jas) □ Q4 (ond) □		Jan-jun □ Jul-dec □		Jan – dec □
5.	Pro-actively asked for any new task from your manager	Jan □ Apr □ Jul □ Oct □	Feb □ May □ Aug □ Nov □	Mar □ Jun □ Sep □ Dec □	Q1 (jfm) □ Q2 (amj) □ Q3 (jas) □ Q4 (ond) □		Jan-jun □ Jul-dec □		Jan – dec □
6.	Actively participated in Company's Program events	Jan □ Apr □ Jul □ Oct □	Feb □ May □ Aug □ Nov □	Mar □ Jun □ Sep □ Dec □	Q1 (jfm) □ Q2 (amj) □ Q3 (jas) □ Q4 (on) □		Jan-jun □ Jul-dec □		Jan – dec □

7.	Pro-actively taken any responsibility	Jan ☐	Feb ☐	Mar ☐	Q1 (jfm) ☐	Jan-jun ☐	Jan – dec ☐
		Apr ☐	May ☐	Jun ☐	Q2 (amj) ☐	Jul-dec ☐	
		Jul ☐	Aug ☐	Sep ☐	Q3 (jas) ☐		
		Oct ☐	Nov ☐	Dec ☐	Q4 (ond) ☐		
8.	Any major achievements	Jan ☐	Feb ☐	Mar ☐	Q (jfm) ☐	Jan-jun ☐	Jan – dec ☐
		Apr ☐	May ☐	Jun ☐	Q2 (amj) ☐	Jul-dec ☐	
		Jul ☐	Aug ☐	Sep ☐	Q3 (jas) ☐		
		Oct ☐	Nov ☐	Dec ☐	Q4 (ond) ☐		
9.	Learned new skill	Jan ☐	Feb ☐	Mar ☐	Q1 (jfm) ☐	Jan-jun ☐	Jan – dec ☐
		Apr ☐	May ☐	Jun ☐	Q2 (amj) ☐	Ju -dec ☐	
		Jul ☐	Aug ☐	Sep ☐	Q3 (jas) ☐		
		Oct ☐	Nov ☐	Dec ☐	Q4 (ond) ☐		

*Initial letters of each month is used as an abbreviation for convenience

*Initial letters of each month is used as an abbreviation for convenience

Start writing here/selecting the checkbox every time you undertake any new responsibility or accept new task on below sheet and be sure to also mention the outcome. This will help you easily keep a track of your activities performed in the previous year along with timelines & details.

Sr.	Date	New task	Description	Outcome
JAN				
FEB				
MAR				
APR				
MAY				
JUN				
JUL				
AUG				
SEP				
OCT				
NOV				
DEC				

Summary

Set your priorities and goals. Categorize them into short- and long-term targets. What you do about your life says a lot about who you are. Accept a new mission, a new responsibility, and provide assistance. To thrive in life, you must be continually changing, which means unlearning old 'rules,' relearning current pieces, and doing more of what makes you feel alive. Some people work on autopilot, repeating the same tasks over and over that didn't work the day before. They are stuck in a loop. They almost never fail to consider the impact of their decisions on themselves instead others, as well as how those actions affect their general well-being. Keep track of your work in a booklet, worksheet, or other text or in the activity checklist cum tracker as mentioned in the previous point. The most straightforward approach is to print the tracker checklist and pin it to your desk. Don't put it in a file or cover it somewhere. And keep updating it each time you start a new activity, complete a mission, provide assistance to someone on your team, or learn a new ability that will be helpful in your next role.

Ch:4 The Opportunity

—Try to keep your mind open to possibilities and your mouth closed on matters that you don't know about. Limit your always and your Never.

– Amy Poehler

Smart people sometimes ask silly questions, ignoring the fact that no question is completely stupid. I've seen people seeking permission politely to ask a dumb question, such as, "Can I ask one silly/stupid question please?" And trust me when I say that the respondent has never refused anything. In fact, this will help you feel a bit more comfortable while asking for your (stupid) question, which you might think is stupid from your viewpoint but may not be from the perspective of others. Don't worry about why you're asking questions; just keep asking until you understand the meaning. According to one wise guy, there are only two circumstances in which you can not pose a question: (i) you are totally sure about the meaning, or (ii) you are completely confused about the context and   are definitely hoping that you will learn/ understand/ clarify your questions by discussing it with your friend or peer present with you in that meeting after the session. Don't be afraid.

Learn to see the usual in the exceptional. Think of progress, not perfection. If you give a precise look, you will find opportunities around you. Identify those before someone else does. Try to find out a difficult task which can be simplified. If you can't find any opportunity, then create one!

4.1 <u>Find your —Why?</u>

—The sky is the limit. You never have the same experience twice.

- Frank McCourt

Over the time, we will be more comfortable with our new way of living and can gradually we'll let go of each one of those beliefs that have kept us stuck and miserable, sometimes for decades. I had never thought of becoming an author but it happened! I opened my mind to accept new possibilities and it felt like everything fell in its right place in its own time.

Let me share my personal experience with you all, I have seen many professionals struggling to get promoted at work and struggling to the better salary raise at work; that too after working hard throughout the year. Hence, I have decided to help these professionals by spreading my message through a medium of my books and the book will contain my detailed analysis and experiences of working in the corporate world.

So my readers don't have to spend these many years to gain this knowledge.

In my debut book —Grow Your Paycheck|, I have revealed the effective strategies to uplift your professional career by improving your credibility and worthiness at your work and to make you one of the most dependable employees in your organization. The steps that I have narrated in my book are in the form of chapters that will make you re-think about your existing stand in your organization.

Once you have envisaged yourself, you should follow your plan of action. Ensure that all of your actions are strategically planned and going in the correct direction and you will achieve your goals in the very near future. Based on my professional experience of working in a corporate environment for over 15+ years, I have written the steps that are widely accepted and followed across the world by working professionals in various organizations.

After reading my book ―Grow Your Paycheck‖, you will change the way you think, feel, act, and behave in your corporate environment.

You will learn:
•*Effective Strategies to advance up your professional career*
•*Improvise your credibility & Worthiness*
•*Boost your performance*
•*Stay in LIMELIGHT in your job and*
•*ULTIMATELY increase your chances of GROWING YOUR PAYCHECK*

If you haven't read it, here is the link to buy it.
[https://amzn.to/3bLot7f]

Hence, my ‗why' behind becoming an author is to help as many professionals as I can to climb their corporate ladder, get promoted at work and simultaneously increase their salary.

4.2 <u>Putting an end to the myths</u>

—The limit of your present understanding is not the limit of your possibilities.

— Guy Finley

I was finally physically prepared to take on a new project that would benefit others. I personally felt that I had too much to give the world and that I could transcend my feelings of being underutilized, limited, and undervalued with everything I bring to the table. As a result, I've wanted to use my experience to affect people and support them in some way.

Following that, I began connecting with my soul and identifying my core skills in which I can assist others so that they do not have to wait as long as I did to learn this experience. Finally, I came to the conclusion that in order to change one's life, one must develop patterns that would inevitably transform into long-term behaviors. I started to unearth old convictions that I had developed and held in my head for many years but had never realized.

They were revealed, and I had the option of going on and working towards them or staying trapped where I was. And I've chosen to take on a new opportunity in order to reach my objectives and started writing.

Hence, I was able to share my all my learning with my readers through my book, which I never thought I would do. Again, I never thought of becoming an author, however, the moment I had decided to help others professionals through medium of my writings by sharing my experiences, I became an author.

I identified the opportunity of people struggling to get good salary raise & getting promoted, hence I started acting on providing assistance in the best possible manner that I could, through my books.

Sometimes, you only need the correct advice and then you'll find your path to success.

4.3 <u>Bridge the gap.</u>

—If you have ideas, you have the main asset you need, and there isn't any limit to what you can do with your business and your life. Ideas are any man's greatest asset.

– Harvey S. Firestone

ZOMATO started with idea of saving time by maintaining multiple menu cards of different restaurants in a softcopy on a website and once they started getting more visitors they've renamed their brand and built a mobile application to make it a convenient and easy access to the users.

Short overview of ZOMATO: Deepinder Goyal and Pankaj Chaddah were the alumni of IIT Delhi and were the employees of Bain & Co in New Delhi. In their office, they came across many people waiting for a long time just to acquire a flash of the menu card. *This is when the idea of obtaining a solution was planted in their mind and that has led to the origination of „Foodiebay'.*

Soft copies of the menu cards were posted to the internet, and after that, everyone in their office started to use this feature, which saved them a lot of time. As a result, their website's traffic improved. They quickly extended their website to make it accessible to the general public. Foodiebay began in Delhi, and its services were later expanded to cities such as Mumbai and Kolkata. The number of users who use the app has been steadily increasing with each passing year. Foodiebay has grown in popularity as a result of its exclusive offerings to consumers.

Foodiebay's designers have been able to scale the idea to an international level as a result of this. Following that, Foodiebay was renamed 'Zomato' to make it more enticing, easy to remember, and to avoid confusion with the website eBay. Zomato was formally known as Foodiebay.

UBER started with a concept of booking a cab (taxi) from a mobile application and saving the time instead of waiting for an unoccupied (available) cab to hire and to be on boarded by its users.

Short overview of UBER: Travis Kalanick and Garrett Camp were attending a conference in Paris in 2008. The duo was searching for a cab one night during the conference but couldn't find one, which made them realize that getting a taxi when needed is such a challenge, and any technology that makes the process easier would undoubtedly be a success. However, the original proposal was for a timeshare limo service, in which a limousine *(a luxury sedan car)* would be shared by several owners.

Since returning to San Francisco, Camp continued to muse on the proposal and even purchased the domain name UberCab.com.

Camp and his friends Oscar Salazar and Conrad Whelan designed the first UberCab concept until mid-2009. After that, Camp confronted Kalanick about joining UberCab. UberCab's service was first tested in New York in early 2010 with just three cabs.

Hence, the popular food deliver company **ZOMATO** and the popular taxi booking company **UBER** have identified the opportunities and a gap that can be filled.

4.4 <u>Take firm decision and inform your management of your desire to get promoted</u>.

—If you limit your choices only to what seems possible or reasonable, you disconnect yourself from what you truly want, and all that is left is compromise.

– Robert Fritz

People excel in life largely because they have a specific goal in mind, have dedicated all of their energy, willpower, efforts, and money to achieving that goal, and have left no stone unturned in achieving that goal. Success isn't just a wishful thinking; it's a blend of imagination and execution. Make a firm determination, define the targets, and continue moving in the best direction toward reaching them. Don't hesitate or backtrack, and remember to never give up.

4.5 <u>Improve the skills</u>

—Maybe other people will try to limit me, but I don't limit myself.

— Jim Carrey

Choose a field of which none of the team members has vast expertise. Spend the time to become an expert in rigorous learning in that area. Your colleagues will learn to rely on you for any insight or solution in that forte, and you will have established a new task or duty. Get yourself valuable. The value and influence of good communication and soft skills will be addressed in the following chapter.

Summary

In a nutshell, try to come up with any creative ways to fill any gaps you can find. It is the only way to succeed and conquer the world. To solve a problem, recognize the potential and work out the simplest way to complete the task. The **Zomato** and **Uber** examples above convey a clear message: -if you encounter any challenging situation in your life, try to simplify it. This will benefit not only you, but others as well, and you will be rewarded for your efforts.

Ch:5 The Right Skills

5.1 Effective communication

Right skills can help you make a splash, elevate your self-esteem, enhance your personal brand, and lead to what we're all looking for −*greater success in every part of our lives.*

Communication skills are vital, no matter what role you hold or how senior you are. When there is a contact failure the results, morale, and priorities also drops. In today's fast-paced job market, organizational communication skills are in high demand, with recruiters looking for candidates that can effectively relay knowledge, negotiate, and work with consumers. Listening intently, clearly, and putting people at ease are all excellent qualities to possess.

Many careers (job titles) demands employees to have outstanding communication skills, which include the ability to express themselves in a positive and coherent fashion both orally and in writing. Communication is one of the most critical facets of business development, but the term "good communication skills" is so overused that it's difficult to describe precisely what it means. Being able to relay information to others in a simple and unambiguous way is a hallmark of strong communication skills.

It involves the easy and straightforward communication process in a way that interacts with the general public. Understanding instructions, mastering new skills, making requests, answering questions, and easily sharing information are all part of effective communication. Good communication skills are one of the most basic characteristics you should have as an employee, but they are also one of the most sought-after by employers.

Understanding requests, answering questions, and relaying main information are all necessary components of successful communication.

Effective collaboration entails more than just exchanging information. It's all about decrypting the feelings and motives that lie underneath the numbers. You must be able to accurately communicate facts as well as listen in order to grasp the whole sense of what is said and to make the other person feel heard and understood.

Effective contact seems to be a natural instinct. Yet, all too much, as we want to communicate with others, something goes wrong. One of the things we mean is that the other party hears something wrong, resulting in misunderstandings, confusion, and confrontation. This will cause problems in your home, education, and work too.

I used to play a game in my school in which, there exists 5-7 participants and the teacher shares a lengthy message consisting of 4-5 sentences to the first participant and that individual has to share the same message received from the teacher to the next participant and the chain continues until it reaches the last participant, which in-turn shall convey the message heard from the previous participant to his/her teacher. Believe me, the intent of the message not only got shredded but got changed in its entirety.

The moral here is, how effective you hear, listen, and pay attention can be gauged by your future actions. In order to get the accurate outcome, you must pay sincere attention to the message & seek clarification if you are uncertain about any point shared by the speaker.

Be sure you're communicating well

For all of us, being able to connect more clearly and easily necessitates the learning of such useful skills. Learning these skills will expand your relationships with others, gain more trust and gratitude, and increase teamwork, problem-solving, and overall social and emotional health whether you're trying to strengthen interaction with your family, infant, boss, or colleagues.

The following are well-known hurdles to efficient communication:

1. **Fear and thoughts of being out of control (losing your cool)**. When you're depressed or emotionally drained,

you're more likely to misinterpret others, send conflicting or nonverbal signals, and engage in unhealthy knee-jerk reactions. You can learn how to quickly calm off before the dialogue starts to avoid confrontation and misunderstanding.

2. **There isn't a lot of focus.** You can't communicate well when you're multitasking. You're almost guaranteed to ignore non-verbal signs in a conversation if you're watching your phone, planning what you're going to say next, or daydreaming. To communicate successfully, you must remove distractions and stay centered.

3. **Inconsistent body language**. Nonverbal communication should validate rather than contradict what has been said. Your viewer is likely to think you're deceiving them if you say one thing but your body language says something else. You can't say "yes" by shaking your head in the east and west

direction. Similarly, you can't say NO by shaking your head in the north and south directions. Try it once, it will be difficult, not impossible, but it will be difficult.

4. **Becoming a Conscious Listener**

   We also understand what we might mean in social contexts. Effective communication, on the other hand, is more about listening than talking. Listening well means not only knowing the words or data being conveyed, but also the emotions that the speaker is trying to share.

5. **Negative expression of your body**.

   You may use disrespectful body language to refute the other person's message if you don't agree with or appreciate what they think, such as folding your arms, looking away, or shaking your legs. You don't have to agree with or even like what's said, but it's important to resist sending derogatory messages in order to communicate effectively and prevent putting the other side on the defensive.

There is a big contrast between engaged listening and actually hearing. When you pay attention to what is being said, you can hear the subtle intonations of someone's voice that tell you how the person feels and the emotions they are trying to express. You can not only understand the other person better if you are a devoted listener, but you will also change the other person.

While communicating in this way, you'll actually go through a process that reduces stress and facilitates physical and emotional well-being. If the person you're interacting with is calm, for example, careful listening will make you relax as well. Similarly, by listening attentively and helping the individual feel heard, if the person is agitated, you can help to relax them.

If the aim is to genuinely understand and interact with the other person, careful listening will always come naturally. The more you practice them, the more satisfying and enjoyable your interactions with others can become.

5.2 <u>Tips on being an active listener in the communication</u>

1. **Pay kind attention (entirely) on the speaker**. You can't listen in an interesting way if you're always checking your phone or worried about something else. You must stay concentrated on the moment-to-moment encounter in order to pick up on subtle nuances and critical nonverbal signs in a conversation. If you're having trouble concentrating on those voices, try repeating their sentences in your head. This will help you stay concentrated.

2. **Listen with your right ear.** As unusual as it might seem, the primary memory regions for both speech comprehension and emotions are found on the left side of the brain. Since the left side of the brain is connected to the right side of the body, using the right ear would help you to feel the emotional nuances of what someone is doing.

3. **Quit bothering people or trying to sway the conversation to your side.** Waiting for your turn to talk is not the same as listening. "If you think that's terrible, let me tell you what happened to me," for example. You can't dwell on what anyone else did while you're shaping what you're going to say next. The speaker will even read your facial expressions and realize that your thoughts are elsewhere and you aren't connected or interested in his talks.

4. **Demonstrate that you're involved in what's being said.** Nod, smile at the person on occasion, and maintain an open and accepting posture. Encourage the speaker to begin with short verbal comments such as "yeah" or "uh huh."

5. **Try to put your individual judgments aside.** To engage with others successfully, you don't have to like them or agree with their ideas, opinions, or points of view. You must, however, set aside your viewpoint and refrain from

blaming or insulting them in order to fully respect them. When executed correctly, the most difficult communication will also result in an accidental connection with others.

6. **Help in receiving reviews.** If there seems to be a dis-connect use paraphrasing to reflect what was said. "*All I think is,*" or "*Sounds like what you think,*" is a perfect way to communicate. But don't just repeat what the speaker said verbatim; you'll come off as insincere or uninformed. Instead, say what the speaker's words mean to you. Ask questions to answer those things, such as "*What do you mean when you say...*" or "*Is that what you're getting at?*"

5.3 Most important communication skills:

1. Emotional Intelligence

Emotional intelligence is the ability to think about and regulate your emotions in order to effectively engage with others, avoid stress, overcome conflicts, and empathize with others. *It's a skill that must be learned rather than acquired over time.* Self-awareness, self-control, social awareness, and intimacy management are the four core components of emotional intelligence. Each of these strands is vital in its own right, helping you to confidently communicate with a range of people.

2. Crisp & Clear speech

The tone of your voice will set the tone of the conversation. If you start the discussion with something insulting or unhelpful, the recipient is more likely to respond in kind. The tone of your voice can be influenced by the level of emotion you use, the strength you use, and the level of touch you use. The same sentence will have a somewhat different meaning depending on which words are emphasized and how the speaker speaks. In a consumer complaint scenario, for example, the tone of voice should be as calm as possible, since an unfriendly tone of voice will only lead to further damage the situation instead of resolving it.

3. Empathy

Everyone has their own ideas of how things can be done in a crowded workplace. Even, if you disagree with your peers or associates, you should consider and respect their point of view. Patience comes in handy when negotiating customer-facing roles with customers. The goal here is to understand where the other person comes from and to respect their perspectives, even though their opinion varies with yours.

4. Listening

Listening properly is the secret to having a productive discussion. Take the time to listen and pay attention to what the other person is thinking and doing. Pay attention to what the other person is saying, ask questions and explain things, and repeat what they've said to ensure that you've interpreted them right.

5. Cohesion and Clarity

It's more than about doing the right thing when it comes to effective communication; it's about communicating thoughts clearly and concisely. Consider what the object of the correspondence is and what data you hope to collect as a result before beginning a call, typing an email, or starting a discussion. Uncertainty and poor decisions will lead to a lack of continuity and cohesion.

6. Friendliness

In any sort of discussion, make sure you set the right tone. People would be able to communicate with you if you use an optimistic sound. Often make an effort to personalize communications, particularly when communicating with friends or coworkers. Always try to personalize your posts, emails, and communication letters instead of simply shooting them out.

7. Respect

Empathy progresses to the next competence in conversation, appreciation. They would be more likely to interact with you if you value others' thoughts and viewpoints. It may both be beneficial to listen actively or clearly use the name of the entity you are listening to. Make sure you don't sound insincere or compose in a manner that is insincere when you type emails.

8. Active Mindfulness

Empathy contributes to the next conversational competency, respect. If you respect other people's opinions and experiences, they would be more likely to communicate with you. Listening consistently or simply mentioning the name of the person you are listening to will also be helpful. When composing letters, make sure you don't sound insincere or write in an insincere way.

9. The faith

In all partnerships, trust (but not arrogance) is important. Clients will have confidence in your abilities to supply what they require and in your ability to deliver on your promises if you show trust. It may be as simple as establishing eye contact during a meeting or speaking to people on the phone in a firm yet respectful tone to express confidence. Be vigilant not to offend someone, or what you plan to do would have the opposite effect.

10. Asking open-ended questions

Strong open-ended questions will help to keep the discussion going and optimize the results. During a conversation, it is normal to ask open-ended questions. There are several questions with prompts that encourage the recipient to address the points and require more specific responses. If you need more details, you can use probing questions like 'Tell me the method of...' to press the receiver to share more information. Throughout the interview, ask a number of questions, including explanations, "what if" situations, and "open-ended questions" to ensure that you fulfill what you set out to do at the start of the call or discussion.

5.4 <u>Soft skills.</u>

Develop your willingness to work under pressure and under a short schedule. Many occupations have tight deadlines and, in some cases, high stakes. Candidates with a decisive mentality, an unwavering willingness to reason straight, and the ability to compartmentalize and put tension aside are respected by the management.

1. **Flexibility**

   Flexibility is a desirable soft skill because it shows the desire and readiness to consider new assignments and challenges with ease. Employees who are versatile are able to chip in when appropriate, take on new duties, and adjust easily when plans change. Employers prefer applicants who can display an optimistic, upbeat outlook and who are unfazed by transition.

2. **Negotiation and Conflict Resolution**

   Another of the soft qualities that managers look for in future leaders is this one. To be a professional negotiator, you must be able to convince and exercise leverage while sensitively finding a solution that favors   the parties concerned. Conflict resolution, too, necessitates good communications abilities and the ability to develop rapport with coworkers and customers alike.

3. Decisiveness

The willingness to make swift and successful decisions characterizes decisiveness. It does not indicate rashness or impulsivity.

Decisiveness combines several different abilities:

- The ability to put things into perspective,
- Weigh up the options,
- Assess all relevant information,
- Anticipate any consequences, good and bad.

When under pressure, a decisive employee will take quick, successful, and well-considered action. They assume responsibility for the consequences of their actions and are able to learn about their mistakes. This prevents chances from being lost due to in-depth analysis or argument.

4. **Time management** is inextricably connected to the ability to operate under duress and to meet strict deadlines. Employees who successfully control their time will plan assignments and coordinate their schedules while keeping a healthy mindset that encourages them to take on additional tasks and deadlines.

5. **Problem Solving**

   Problem solving necessitates not only logical, imaginative, and rational thinking abilities, but also a certain mindset; those who can approach a problem with a calm, clear head will always arrive at a solution more quickly than those who cannot. This is a soft ability that often depends on good coordination. Problems do not necessarily have to be solved by themselves. Knowing who can support you with finding a solution and how they can do it can be immensely helpful.

6. **Responsibility**

   Responsibility is a soft skill that is barely addressed but highly regarded. Colleagues who struggle to take care of their jobs would be less effective and successful in the long term. Be sure you can learn these skills and show a high degree of accountability:

- Trustworthiness
- Discipline
- Motivation
- Conscientiousness
- Accountability

Taking action entails taking care of not just your own priorities, but also the objectives of the organization as a whole. This would include taking the initiative to change the situation, admitting blame for any mistakes, and genuinely worrying for your future.

7. Leadership

Leadership is a soft trait that you can exhibit even though you are not in control of others. Many leaders who possess good leadership abilities would be able to motivate others and guide teams to success. This is why it is such a sought-after skill.

People with strong leadership abilities can possess a variety of skills that will be helpful in the workplace, including:

- A positive attitude and outlook,
- The ability to make quick and effective decisions,
- Exemplary problem-solving or conflict management skills,
- The ability to communicate effectively,
- An aptitude for both self-motivating and motivating others.

And if you're applying for an entry-level role, don't be shy to prove your talent by demonstrating how you've already motivated others to complete a job.

8. Self-Motivation

In today's world, possessing a good outlook and the initiative to work effectively without continuous supervision is a necessary soft skill for any employee. It not only illustrates dependability and dedication, but it also demonstrates that you can work well within an organizational system without continuous oversight. Find these primary qualities to show your inspiration:

- Positivity
- Ambition
- Commitment
- Initiative

9. Teamwork

Effective coordination, like leadership, necessitates the use of a variety of soft skills. Acting as part of a team to accomplish a shared purpose necessitates the intuition and leadership abilities to know when to lead and when to listen. Perceptive and sensitive to the wishes and responsibilities of others are qualities of good team players, and they are dedicated in their work.

10. Communication

One of the most essential soft skills is communication. Ability communicators may adapt their sound and style to their audience, grasp and respond on orders quickly, and explain difficult topics to coworkers and customers. Listening is an essential communication trait that is frequently overlooked. Your verbal and nonverbal talents are equally essential. Verbal skills are essential for cultivating constructive, respectful, and eventually fruitful relationships.

This is true with the handwritten communication as well. Since so much business correspondence now takes place by email, it's essential to know proper email etiquette to have directions that are transparent and succinct.

5.5 <u>Strong Interpersonal Skills</u>

Every day, we use leadership techniques. Interpersonal abilities (*in a professional context*) relate to how we communicate with others and are closely related to emotional intelligence. Interpersonal skills become more relevant as you step into the workforce. Many soft skills may be categorized as interpersonal, and they are all used in the workplace to varying degrees based on where you work and the level of duty. Employers also search out applicants with outstanding leadership skills. They aggressively recruit candidates who can operate in a team environment, connect efficiently, and establish good interactions with consumers and colleagues. Self-confidence, collaboration and positivity are all interpersonal skills much in demand.

What is the importance of Interpersonal Skills?
Nearly all facets of employment need coordination, daily business will be very complicated without interpersonal skills. Many roles require teamwork and contact with a variety of individuals from different divisions & locations, and interpersonal skills are required to do so. Even if you work in a highly technical area, such as IT, you will often communicate with peers or customers, either conveying nuanced details or paying close attention to specifications. Having outstanding technological skills on your resume isn't often enough to get you a career.

Strong Interpersonal Skills include:

1. *Self-Reliance*
2. *Regulation of Partnerships*
3. *Feedback receptivity*
4. *Ethics at Jobs*
5. *Regulation of Disputes*
6. *Body Language*
7. *Etiquette for Office*
8. *Collaboration*
9. *Listening*
10. *Strong stance (positivity at work)*
11. *Develop a Positive Attitude*

Let"s see these skills in detail:

1. Self-Reliance

The right level of organizational self-assurance will help you win recognition and open doors. It will also explain how you manage multiple situations and how you deal with them effectively and efficiently. It is critical to show self-confidence at any stage in your career, whether you are a newcomer looking for an entry position or a more experienced team member looking for promotion. People will like you better if you have self-confidence at work, and they will take your ideas, advice, and views more seriously. When working with people, their trust will help you because it will allow you to better articulate yourself and be heard.

2. Regulation of Partnerships

It's one thing to shape fruitful alliances, but it's quite another to keep them moving. This is a crucial asset in a variety of positions, from entry-level to management. In every level of an organization, you would be forced to interact with colleagues, partners, and clients. The opportunity to sustain relationships based on mutual respect and shared trust is critical in every business environment.

3. Feedback receptivity

Being sensitive to criticism would help you develop both socially and professionally. View all feedback as a motivation to improve, and never take it personally. This can take some time, particularly if the feedback is harsh, but try to take a deep breath and find ways on how you can improve yourself in those areas. To get on-board feedback, you must first listen to it. Don't consider your response; instead, pay attention to what they're doing. Take what you've gained and bring it to good use to increase your performance and productivity.

4. Ethics at Jobs

Most recruiters look favorably on candidates who have a strong work ethic. But, what does a career ethic have to do with it? Okay, it can be divided into three distinct strands:

- **Professionalism** - This covers everything from how you present yourself and communicate with others to your personal presence.

- **Respect** - Workplaces need you to work under duress at some stage, and exhibiting grace under duress will help you achieve further respect. Regardless of how close the deadline is or how hot the situation gets, diplomacy and poise are preserved.

- **Dependability** - Employers identify this quality this beforehand so that they can rely on their staff. This reflects your work ethic and dedication to the industry by being well organized and doing the job while you are already on time, i.e. when you said you will.

5. Regulation of Disputes

Regulation of Conflicts, also known as conflict management, is a valuable organizational skill for those serving in teams, particularly for those pursuing leadership roles. Confrontation in the workplace can reduce productivity and build negativity. Good crisis management capabilities include diplomacy, empathy, negotiation, assertiveness, and agreement. Being able to articulate one or defend others' points of view in a respectful and courteous way is a highly required skill in the workplace.

6. Body Language

Nonverbal communication is often ignored, so bear in mind how the body language and gestures can be interpreted. Variables to include when interacting with others include:

- Touch with the eye
- Expressions of Facial
- Gestures
- In-person room
- Posture and the location of the body

Your body language will influence how your verbal speech (words) is perceived. In practice, your body language has a greater effect on your communication skills than any other factor.

7. Etiquette for Office

How you come across to someone will say about yourself at first glance. It gives an opportunity to someone to build an image of your personality or behavior in their mind before they act. Organizing office manners is a smart way to make a lasting impression on anyone you meet. Check the pose, make sure you're standing tall and making eye contact, and turn to people as they chat and give them a friendly smile. Accept the company's dress code to ensure that the clothes, such as shoes, coat, purse, and jewelry, are suitable for the workplace. Make sure you display wisdom and courtesy and that you report at work on time every day.

8. Collaboration

Collaborative work allows people to work together productively to create positive outcomes for customers and the company. Successful teamwork necessitates a desire to collaborate and trust one another. Employers often favor candidates who have a demonstrated track record of working successfully as part of a team, as well as applicants who will cooperate and partner to deliver excellent results. When interviewing for a job, being able to work together is a big bonus, especially in tough situations. Present yourself and your enthusiasm for teamwork with a positive attitude.

9. Listening

When it comes to strengthening your interpersonal speech skills, the first lesson to note is to listen. Failure to listen closely may have terrible results, ranging from failure to obey a boss's instructions or to failing to complete a client's order. Active listening is the ability to hear and learn from others, as well   as respond respectfully to what they say. Giving nonverbal cues that you are actively listening to *(such as nodding or sustaining eye contact)* will raise morale and you will be heard by your colleagues.

10. Strong stance (positivity at work)

Even in difficult situations, it is important to have a positive attitude. Be upbeat from the time you apply your resume or write a cover letter to the interview, the first day on the job, and beyond. Never say something bad about your new or ex employer, no matter how badly you feel about it. Employees with a constructive outlook are more likely to see each other in the same way, resulting in a more harmonious workplace.

11. Develop a Positive Attitude

In the workplace, having the appropriate level of self-confidence would unlock doors and encourage you to achieve attention. It will also explain how you manage and interact with a variety of scenarios in a constructive and successful way. To be successful, you must show self-confidence at any point of your career, whether you are a novice searching for an entrance position or a more seasoned team member looking for advancement. Self-confidence at work will improve people's perceptions of you, and they will take your ideas, suggestions, and viewpoints more seriously. When communicating with others, faith means that you will share yourself openly and that you will be understood.

Summary

Changing the game always requires YOU making the necessary adjustments. Recognition of one's true self is the path to happiness. Invest in your professional growth, improve your skills, and don't skip on your education. Communication, soft skills, and leadership skills are all attributes that employers search for, as I discussed earlier in this chapter. Study, learn, and you'll be able to master these abilities over time. Your right learning can bear more fruits for you, and for a longer period of time. And, as one wise man once said, "*No intelligence is ever wasted*."

Ch:6 The Arrangement

—Everything you've ever wanted is on the other side of fear.

– George Addair

Think confidently and you'll be able to conquer your fears. During their fear, most people realize their true ability, and then they experience the joy of fulfilling their objectives. Don't just sit there, do something! In no circumstance can you allow your fear to rule your life. Know that the anxiety is only temporary, but if you do not resolve it at the proper moment, you will regret it any time you recall the situation. Rather, overcome your apprehension by being bold and taking on the daunting mission or circumstance. The worst that can happen is that you don't excel, but you won't have the regret of failure to try at least once. At the end of the task, you will have either found a better way to execute the task or dealt with the problem, or you will have accomplished your task successfully. Whatever happens, you've taken a step away from your present position, which is a positive thing. Let me explain the Cause and Effect Rules to you. Nothing occurs by accident or beyond the Fundamental Rules, according to it. Any behavior is scrutinized for this statute. This is because every action has a corresponding response, and every action has an effect, and we reap what we have sown.

6.1   Start building your brand by taking responsibilities.

—Everything you can imagine is real.
— Pablo Picasso

The more people who argue about an issue, the less change is made. Take a step back and consider creative solutions to the situation. The business becomes extremely successful once you become a problem solver. When attempting to answer difficult questions, speak with others as well. It improves your chances of success as you work to build confidence in your team. Plus, when a problem occurs that necessitates further accountability, people tend to consider you as the "go-to" man. The more you disparage a person or situation, the more important your rapport becomes. Complainers should not be encouraged, regardless of the merits of their arguments.

6.2   <u>Don't be afraid while asking for</u> <u>new duties and deliver results</u>

—Don't worry about failures, worry about the chances you miss when you don't even try.

— Jack Canfield

If you wanted a promotion at work, the only way to get it was to take the initiative. "*Take on the job. Get the part.*" That is, planning to do some of the work involved with the next assignment while trying to do the current work was the best way to receive the next promotion. That's how you'll be remembered by management and show to them that you're worthy of a raise. This comes from the assumption that the organization holds the work, however you own the future.

6.3   Lead by example.

—Great minds discuss ideas; average minds discuss events; small minds discuss people.

– Eleanor Roosevelt

One of this management style's distinguishing characteristics is team skill-sharing, in which workers are expected to focus on and learn from one another rather than just their boss. Managers will also assist direct reports by offering strategic projects and forums for them to demonstrate their talents and ideas. According to Michael Canic, a policy and execution specialist, there are three items a leader must do to achieve effectively:

    i.   cultivate the right focus,
    ii.   establish the right environment, and
    iii.   construct the right team.

It won't matter whether you have the right emphasis or the right atmosphere if you don't have the right team ""Every corporate touchpoint is regularly matched with your focus in the right environment," Canic says. As a consequence, a philosophy of commitment and success emerges. A leader should do five things to build the right atmosphere.

1. Connecting the dots.

People must be instilled with a sense of mission in order to be engaged. However, having a goal in mind isn't enough. Translating the intent into corporate goals and individual objectives is often important. As a consequence, intent becomes concrete and actionable.

2. Strategic management, not strategic planning.

Many businesses see regulation as an event rather than a mechanism. The attention moves to the day-to-day requirements after they've established a master plan. Canic recommends that leaders practice strategic leadership, which is a continual process in which the strategy is turned into time-linked milestones and events that are tracked, measured, and supervised.

3. Coach, don't just manage.

Coaches think, "*What can I do to help each team member succeed at their highest level?*" Coaches offer performance reviews and guidance on a daily basis. When goals aren't fulfilled, they keep staff members constructively accountable and emphasize the correct behaviors and results.

4. Equip people to succeed.

People get depressed because they lack the requisite tools. They feel useless because they lack the necessary skills. They don't feel trusted and they don't have enough authority. Instead of setting their people up to struggle, leaders should equip them to succeed. That needs at the very least adequate expertise, abilities, money, and authority.

5. Connect with the heart and the head will follow.

You get optional commitment — the above-and-beyond initiative-taking that increases the organization's capacity to perform — when you show that you value, respect, and care about people as individuals.

6.4 Ask, Accept & Put more on your plate - keep your plate full.

—**Do the one thing you think you cannot do. Fail at it. Try again. Do better the second time. The only people who never tumble are those who never mount the high wire. This is your moment. Own it.**

— Oprah Winfrey

Many tasks mean more exposure and opportunities for the boss to work on projects that are relevant to him. More conference calls, web calls, voice chats, face-to-face sessions, and seminars translate into getting insight to your boss's wider viewpoint, innovative approaches to addressing issues, and ways to show your value. It also makes it easy to request extra funds to finish your tasks and to justify your progress to your supervisors.

Demonstrate to your supervisor that he should delegate vital things to you without having to treat you like a prince. When you take on additional responsibilities or responsibilities within your organization or in cross-functional departments, you end up interacting together with a diverse community of people. Each young person brings new experience and understanding of new opportunities to the career. This is your true business network, and as your connections expand, so does your ability to progress your career.

6.5   <u>Time management & learn the art of saying NO.</u>

—It is never too late to be what you might have been.

— George Eliot

At times, you shall need to be assertive and say 'No' to new responsibilities. You can say no in these following situations:

- *if it's a strategic misfit for the way you want your career to go,*

- *if it's a misfit of the talents you possess or would hope to acquire, otherwise you're going to struggle and*

- *if it's a misfit in your personality, you'll be demotivated instead.*

If you don't have time, don't take in more than you can handle. It's not a smart idea if you're going through a personal challenge or if the new initiative is stopping you from completing   core goals. Remember that every new career would need you to work a few more hours as you practice it. You could also interrupt low-impact activities if you have the bandwidth and capacity. Your actions would be of no benefit if the project is not critical to the success of the company. Instead, if anything big happens, it can obstruct your time and allow you to lose concentration.

Instead, you should concentrate on studying the activities that would be useful in your next role. Identify the additional responsibilities and begin devoting a fixed period of time to mastering them, since this experience will certainly assist you in executing your current duties after you are promoted.

Summary

Make no effort to appease anyone. You are not being rewarded for satisfying anyone. By attempting to please others and striving for acceptance, you would quickly become exhausted. The easiest ways to master skills faster are to learn in depth, try new things, explore solutions, and get help if you get lost. It's the most powerful way to keep track of the experiences that identify you as an individual. There are no fundamental or golden rules that apply. You must learn to make your own rules in order to follow your own path. Life is unpredictably uncertain. It won't everything go according to plan. Prepare for the future such that it does not come as a disappointment.

Ch:7 The Conclusion

Remember, no one is ever prepared for something unless and until he believes that he can achieve it. The first step is to accept it with complete confidence in your mind. Rather than just a hope or wish, your state of mind must contain a strong belief. You must understand that everyone who has amassed great fortunes, achieved success, and won battles did gone through a period of dreaming, hoping, wishing, desiring, and planning. You may be aware that every great leader throughout history, from the dawn of civilization to the present, was a wise dreamer.

7.1   Envision yourself as promoted.

—The Way To Get Started Is To Quit Talking And Begin Doing.

— Walt Disney

It's something athletes do before a big game. It's something soldiers do before they step onto the battlefield. Every day, visionary business leaders do it. This is something that the world's best athletes excel at. When we imagine ourselves achieving a goal of any kind, our brain begins to work out how to make it happen. As you begin to paint a picture of your life as you want it to be, things will continue to shift in that direction. According to Forbes, Karen Mason Riss, a certified professional social worker, says that if you want to improve your life, you should try to visualize it by asking yourself, "*What are the things that I already bring to the table?*" Just because things aren't exactly as you'd like them to be right now doesn't mean you haven't already begun moving in that direction. Make sure you believe in yourself and consider positive thinking. This will assist you in continuing to progress. Make a mental image of yourself and work on it. To be able to articulate how it feels to succeed, develop a mental image of what it feels like to succeed. Consider your training schedule if you want to compete in a marathon of life. Pretend to be a character in the case. Now, whatever you want to do will have an impact on your future. So choose things that will help you become the person you want to be. Consider yourself as you want the outcome to be.

7.2 Keep your results (numbers) handy - refer the annual activities checklist.

—It is our choices that show what we truly are, far more than our abilities.

— J.K.Rowling

We no longer live in a Stone Age. In today's world of neck to neck competition, we must work smart. Those days have gone where people used to get promoted based on the likings by their sr. management or merely by giving fake appreciations and living a life on -yes-mode to any and everything you manager says. Now time has changed. People expect you to talk straight and be transparent. If you can't handle any task or unable to complete any task in the expected timeline then you are expected to buy some additional time to finish that task and in case if you get stuck then you are also free to seek additional assistance from an expert to complete that task.

Stop creating false expectations, it's always better to be upfront with facts rather than hiding it. If you haven't done it in past then it's the right time to accept a new task, take appropriate knowledge transfer training from an expert who has already performed that task with excellence and learn it.

In my opinion, it is the right time prove yourself and get rewarded. No favoritism, no partiality and no dirty politics should ever exist in any organization. I know, regardless of the efforts, such crappy things do exist in many organizations. However; the important thing is, one can still overcome such issues (if any) by proving themselves before their management and build his image in the eyes of his management.

There are two kinds of management, I am not sure if you have heard of it, i.e., *Management by Objective and Management by Results* (also known as objective and key results). For decades, MBO (which stands for "management by goals") has been a common management method. But there is an alternate approach that at the moment is gaining a lot of traction: OKR (or "goals and key results/outcomes").

Management by Objective (MBO): In his 1954 book, The Art of Management, MBO was proposed by Peter Drucker as a means to boost organizational efficiency. In essence, MBO outlines a framework for workers to identify concrete and consistent priorities and is intended to create a culture of working against shared organizational objectives. The idea has spread globally, and has become the "norm" for many businesses. Indeed, if you think of the traditional way of performance management, i.e. a manager agrees with each employee's expectations, and then their performance (and compensation) is measured against these targets, what you're aware of is **MBO**.

Management by Results (OKR): That at the moment, it is gaining a lot of coverage, and has been popularized by tech giants such as Google, you might assume that OKR is a modern solution. OKR has been around for decades, in fact. Andrew Grove, the former CEO of Intel, introduced the idea in the early 1980s and caught the attention of John Doerr, a venture capitalist (and early Google investor). From his time at Intel, Doerr picked up the approach and took it to Google, which liked it, and OKR expanded from there.

Setting strategic goals is at the root of the OKR strategy, as it is with MBO. It goes further than MBO, however, by dividing policy and development into two parts: objectives (Os) and main outcomes (Os) (the KRs). This simply means that you should set a goal and then figure out how you're going to achieve it.

And what is the actual difference?

OKR arose from MBO, essentially cherry-picking and expanding on some of the better elements of MBO. The MBO and OKR methods are inextricably linked. Finally, in addition to evaluating efficiency, provide a framework for defining and sharing goals. Both motivate people to work toward a common goal.

1. **MBO points out what you intend to do, while OKR sets out what and how to do it.**

The MBO plan is all about figuring out what you want to achieve. It's fairly flexible and transparent in terms of how a person or team achieves that goal and how their performance is measured against that goal.

OKR, on the other hand, goes into even more depth. The key findings define success and, as a result, what needs to be accomplished to complete the task, and these findings are translated into quantitative performance metrics.

2. **MBO is reviewed regularly, while OKR normally takes place periodically.**

MBO works on a regular schedule, setting goals for the next year, which are then revised and updated over the course of the year. I say "traditionally" because the annual review period is no longer appropriate in today's fast-paced world, and many companies are opting to review MBOs more frequently. (In fact, I have no doubt that if Peter Drucker wrote his book today, it would be subjected to more frequent reviews.)

With milestones and results being reviewed, OKR is planned for a shorter period of time, at least quarterly, if not weekly. This allows you to improve the track's productivity by highlighting areas where something might be off track.

3. **MBO, though OKR is public and open, is private and siloed.**

MBO goals are set in a private meeting between an individual and their immediate reporting manager, and the goals are kept secret. Part of the reason for this secrecy is that MBO is linked to reimbursement (which we'll discuss later).

OKRs, on the other hand, seem to be formed through wider team gatherings, with the whole company deciding how to support the larger business's goals. Anyone, from the CEO to the shop floor employees, will be able to see the OKRs of others.

While OKRs, MBOs, and other goal-setting tactics differ, they all lead to the same end result for each employee: accurate, attainable, and applicable targets. Find a schedule that works for your business, stick to it, and reap the benefits of your employees' clear goal-setting.

As a result, I highly advise you to keep all of your reports on hand before approaching your immediate reporting manager and requesting a promotion.

7.3   Timing of promotion

—You're not obligated to win. You're obligated to keep trying to the best you can do everyday.

— Jason Mraz

You should be mindful of the arrangement of your business or your job duties. Some companies have set procedures for promoting its employees, such as at the time of the annual performance evaluation, while others reward their employees depending on the organization's needs and the individual's skills. Some companies, on the other hand, provide promotion with a condition that the candidate obtains the necessary experience and expertise that can be useful to him or her in the next job title before actually being promoted.

As a result, first recognize the issue, then develop a course of action (business case), and finally take action. Simply go for it after you've proven yourself by mastering your assigned duty and you're ready to take on new duties without jeopardizing your current responsibilities (tasks). Request for a promotion!

7.4   <u>Your revised version - 2.0</u>

—**Success comes from knowing that you did your best to become the best that you are capable of becoming.**

— **John Wooden**

To create the life you want, you'll need to make some significant changes in your life. Have faith in yourself and strive for the best life possible. Consider how different your life can be in the next few years if you intend to take care of yourself today. In your life, respect yourself enough to be the founder of your life. Start creating the life you desire, and yes, you do deserve it!

7.5 <u>What if you don't get promoted this year?</u>

Have you put all the reasonable best efforts to get promoted to the next rank at your work? Have you consistently sustained excellence in all of the tasks assigned to you? It would be excruciatingly frustrating if you do not get a promotion this year. You are now free to be emotional during the manager's meeting. You'll get good feedback and a greater understanding of your role within the organization during this period. Each promotion decision must have a justification. As you've seen time and time again, start with a strong business case. There's never a guarantee that you'll get a promotion, but the odds are in your favor. You may then take the advice to modify and then ask again after you've done so in those sectors. If you really believe it is unfair, you may choose to apply for another job in another agency. Remember that your present position or situations are the product of your previous decisions and feelings, and that you have the ability to affect the future based on your current actions. That is not the end of your life; you have already completed half of it, so it will only be another year. Don't give up before you get promoted; remember, you've already made an impact on your boss, so your path to management will be a lot easier this time. Good Luck!

Summary

Any promotion in a company must be defined. You had waited until you had proven yourself in your new role before requesting a promotion. As a result, make sure you have a clear report ready that includes your cumulative yearly achievements, figures, and any additional tasks you did in the past year to improve the success of the company or any team member. You might argue that recruiting you for the next role and providing you with a staff would allow you to focus more on the organization's main initiative. Furthermore, you have shown that you can achieve great outcomes after you are formally elevated, based on the results you have delivered in the previous year without keeping this current title and all of this with such limits and limitations. You'll keep doing what you're doing and you shall continue to deliver success with more zeal at your work.

#How to get the most out of this book

Destiny is not a matter of chance. It's a matter of choices we make. We do not choose to stick on our existing role but we fail to make right choices or make bad decisions to not break our lovely so-called **comfort zone**. Ultimately, life is all about what we make of it consciously through our decisions and actions. If we don't act then that is also our decision that we have decided not to act. So we sadly & quietly settle down with our life the way it flows and carry the feeling of incompleteness throughout our life by giving numerous reasons for not getting success.

Don't just sit in your comfort zone instead step-out. Every person who has succeeded in their life has tried different ways until they achieve their desired goals. If you try then you can succeed, but if you don't try, there is absolutely no way that you can succeed because you always miss **100%** of the chances you don't take. You might continue to experience obstacles or frustrations or difficulties until you change your approach and your behavior or until you do it differently. Sooner or later you will surely learn that you wanted to learn. For some people, it could be a shorter span and for others it could be a longer time but until that person don't quit, he or she will reach his or her desired destination.

Your final step is to make a commitment to yourself. Write this down and put it somewhere in your house where you can daily see it. "*I'm going to dedicate daily one (1) hour for upcoming six months to learn all those new skills that my next position demands.*" That's a small and achievable target. I want you to start there because, when you hit that goal after a month, you can move on to the next one. By having a clear, written down goal and a commitment for the amount of time you'll invest in reaching that goal, the probabilities of you achieving your desired goal seems much closer and achievable. It's the people who don't take this tiny action step and write this down that become failures and start complaining that they didn't had any opportunity to succeed in their life. Download the activity checklist cum tracker sheet as referred in *Chapter 3* (*3.5 track your work*).

Prioritize your one goal to rule all the other goals. There will be distractions but if you make that commitment and start taking action in a strategic manner, success transforms from a ***possibility to certainty.***

Read this book a few times and return to it anytime you feel the need to refresh your memory. It took me over 15+ years of experience in working in the corporate environment to gain the knowledge you now have in this book. The best part is you don't have to invest that many years to discover that knowledge because it's all here in this book. What you have to do now is read this book and put what you've learned into effect.

Not only learn but also master all the new skills (one after another) required for your next role/job title before you are actually being promoted. This way, you will learn new skills and once you are promoted you'll handle these tasks with ease.

#Professional Goals

Instead of waiting for the right time, begin now by writing down your professional goals (both short and long term) and then by following the techniques as described in this book, start progressing in your professional career and accomplish your goals in the near future.

Write your short term professional goals *(while writing your short term goals kindly break down your goals into monthly, quarterly, half-yearly and annually goals):*

Write your Long term professional goals (*while writing your long term goals kindly break down your goals into monthly, quarterly, half-yearly and annually goals*)**:**

#Affirmations

Give yourself a commitment to never give-up on your dreams and constantly learning new skills to achieve success in your professional & personal life. List down the skills that you have ever wished to learn but you could not learn it for some reason. By listing it here, you are giving a strong message to your brain that you haven't given-up on your dreams of learning that new skill for which you have been interested since long. Prioritize it & decide that skill you wish to learn first and then excel in that skill by continuous learning.

Skills I am keen to learn (on priority) which will accelerate my professional career are (in order):

1. _____
2. _____
3. _____
4. _____
5. _____
6. _____
7. _____
8. _____
9. _____
10. _____
11. _____

Credits

https://www.google.com/

https://www.wikipedia.org/

https://everydaypower.com/

https://www.economictimes.com/

https://www.inc.com/

https://www.linkedin.com/

https://startuptalky.com/

https://www.pinterest.com/

https://www.goodreads.com/

https://pixabay.com/ and other webpages

#Disclaimer

Please note the information contained within this document is for educational and entertainment purpose only. All effort has been executed to present accurate, up to date, reliable and complete information. No warranties of any kind are declared or implied.

The aforementioned viewpoints in this book are those of Swapnil Modi. The content of this book deals with various steps and principles to reach a desirable designation in an organization. Many of these steps are widely accepted and followed across the world by working professionals in various organizations. With no intention to endorse someone else's learning as the authors own because the author has shared his learning, truths and beliefs based on his personal experience by working in a corporate world for over 15+ years.

Although the author has made every effort to ensure that the information & strategies in this book turn out as a beneficial guide to his readers in advancing-up their career. However; the author hereby disclaims any liability to any individual or entity, for any loss, damage, or disruption caused by acts or omissions of the readers, whether such acts or omissions resulted by implementing any strategies either expressed or implied, in this book.

By reading this document, the reader agrees that under no circumstances is the author responsible for any losses, direct or indirect, that are incurred as a result of the use of the information contained within this document, including but not limited to, errors, omissions or inaccuracies and nor the author be held liable for any damage caused as a result of you buying, acquiring or reading this book.

This book is a result of the author's personal corporate experience. Despite that, this book is still just a general guide only. How to act in any organization or situation is different and the advice in this book should not be used with your own personal judgment. The reader is responsible for his or her future action. This book makes no guarantees of future success. However, by following the steps that are listed in this book will certainly help you change your perspective towards your professional career.

Readers are strongly advised not to take any adverse action after reading this book as the author's sole intent is to help their readers to grow in their profession and not to damage/hurt their career in any manner whatsoever. Also, the author has given credits to appropriate parties whose quotes and references were used while writing this book and if anyone has been missed out, it could be merely a bona fide error.

#About the author

Mr. Swapnil P. Modi

LL.M. (Gold Medalist), LL.B. (Gold Medalist), and M.B.A. (HR)

The author of this book, **Swapnil Modi** is a dynamic & detailed oriented professional having over 15 years of extensive working experience in corporate world. He has been ranked as **10X STAR PERFORMER** in his professional career with Etech, Inc.

He carries abundant experience in **Reviewing / Drafting / Vetting** on all types of agreements and mitigating risk for his clients. He is an expert in maintaining the highest level of quality in operations; ensuring adherence to all the legal parameters and compliances as per the stringent norms.

He was honored with the **GOLD MEDAL** for RANKING FIRST in Gujarat University Final LL.B Examination & he also was honored with the **"SHIELD & CERTIFICATE"** for RANKING FIRST in MOOT COURT COMPETITION held in Siddharth Law College, Gandhinagar, Gujarat. He holds a FIRST CLASS degree in M.B.A. (HR) from NIMS UNIVERSITY.

His debut book -<u>**Grow Your Paycheck**</u> has hit the **#1 BEST SELLER** in various categories and it's available in multiple languages: English, Hindi, Spanish, Portuguese and French.

Book Link: https://amzn.to/3bLot7f

About my previous book

My dear readers, you might have read my debut book titled as "**Grow Your Paycheck.**" In case, if you have missed it, grab your copy soon.

#Praise for Author

With much appreciation, I want to give you big thanks for buying and reading my book. You could have chosen any other book, but you took mine, and believe me that I honestly appreciate this.

I hope you got at least a few actionable insights on how to scale up your career ladder at work and steps to get promoted to the next rank or job title in the corporate world.

Can I ask for 30 seconds more of your time? I'd love it if you could leave a review of this book. I want to hear from you! Your thoughts and comments are important to me. Reviews may not matter to big named authors, but they immensely help for the rising talent authors like me, with hardly any followings yet. They help me to grow my readership by encouraging folks to take a chance on my books. I read all the reviews personally so that I can get your feedback and make this book even better.

It will just take less than a minute of your time and tremendously help me reach out to more people, so please leave your review on the book review page before you leave.

Thanks again for your support and I'd look forward to see your review.

Connect with the author:

LinkedIn: Click Here To Connect
[Link: https://www.linkedin.com/in/swapnil-modi-64098448/]
Amazon author page: Click Here To Follow
[Link: https://www.amazon.in/Swapnil-Modi/e/B08LC65MK5]
Telegram: **iSmodi365**
Instagram: **iSmodi365**
Twitter: **iSmodi365**
Facebook: Click Here to Connect
[https://www.facebook.com/**ismodi365**]
And email me @ **iSmodi365@gmail.com**

Platform:	Account id:
Telegram	
Instagram	
Twitter	**iSmodi365**
Facebook	
Gmail	

#Thanks Note

I would like to thank all the readers for their support by going through this book. I hope this book helps you to increase productivity as well as enhance your professional personality. When I sit down to write about the ideas or insights I want to share here, there's always a consideration in my mind of how this book can benefit my readers.

With so many wonderful resources and articles out there sharing great content and ideas, I want to make sure that my readers are happy with their decision to spend some of their quality time here on my book and learning the hacks of enhancing their professional career.

All the best,
Mr. Swapnil P. Modi
LL.M (GOLD MEDALIST),
LL.B. (GOLD MEDALIST),
and M.B.A. (HR) .